Wallace & Gromit

Curse of the Were-Rabbit

The Monstrously Scary Joke Book

PUFFIN

Wallace & Gromit

Curse of the Were-Rabbit

THE
MONSTROUSLY SCARY

JOKE BOOK

By Amanda Li

Screenplay by Mark Burton, Bob Baker, Steve Box and Nick Park

PUFFIN BOOKS

Published by the Penguin Group
Penguin Books Ltd, 80 Strand, London WC2R 0RL, England
Penguin Group (USA) Inc., 375 Hudson Street, New York, New York 10014, USA
Penguin Group (Canada), 90 Eglinton Avenue East, Suite 700, Toronto,
Ontario, Canada M4P 2Y3 (a division of Pearson Penguin Canada Inc.)
Penguin Ireland, 25 St Stephen's Green, Dublin 2, Ireland
(a division of Penguin Books Ltd)
Penguin Group (Australia), 250 Camberwell Road, Camberwell, Victoria 3124,
Australia (a division of Pearson Australia Group Pty Ltd)
Penguin Books India Pvt Ltd, 11 Community Centre, Panchsheel Park,
New Delhi – 110 017, India
Penguin Group (NZ), cnr Airborne and Rosedale Roads, Albany,
Auckland 1310, New Zealand (a division of Pearson New Zealand Ltd)
Penguin Books (South Africa) (Pty) Ltd, 24 Sturdee Avenue, Rosebank,
Johannesburg 2196, South Africa

Penguin Books Ltd, Registered Offices: 80 Strand, London WC2R 0RL, England

www.penguin.com

First published 2005
1

Made and printed in England by Clays Ltd, St Ives plc

British Library Cataloguing in Publication Data
A CIP catalogue record for this book is available from the British Library

ISBN 0–141–31887–2

CONTENTS

Beware the Beastly Bunny!   1

The Dynamic Duo   14

The Fearful Food   26

The Vile Victor   40

The Terrified Townsfolk   47

BEWARE THE BEASTLY BUNNY!

In the dead of night, in a tiny town, there's a monster munching its way through the vegetable plots. The annual Giant Vegetable Competition is just days away, but the townsfolk of West Wallaby need to watch out: there's a very hungry Were-rabbit about . . .

What's the most dangerous time to see the Were-rabbit? The twitching hour.

What kind of monster can terrorize an entire village? A great big hare-ey beast.

What's the best way to speak to the Were-rabbit? From a very long distance.

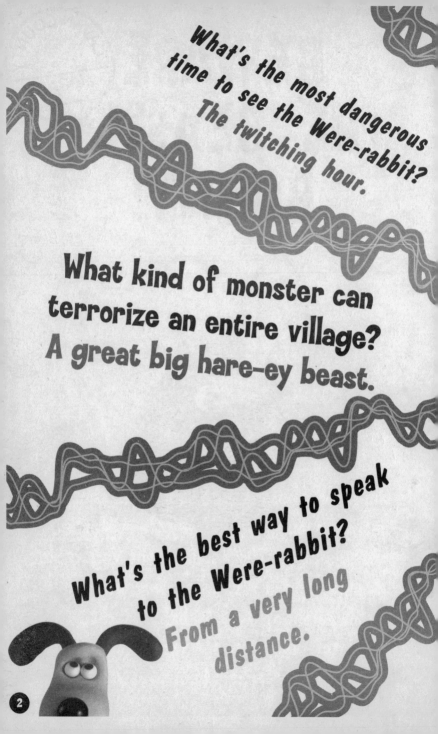

How do you stop the Were-rabbit howling in the back of the car?
Put it in the front.

What should you do if you find the Were-rabbit in your bed?
Sleep in the wardrobe.

Did you hear about the little bunny who wanted to turn into the Were-rabbit? It just wanted a change.

What made the Were-rabbit stop in its tracks? It had to paws for thought.

What did the Were-rabbit do before bed? It read a bite-time story.

Does the Were-rabbit eat everything it's given?

No, it likes to pick and chews.

Did you hear the one about the Were-rabbit's party?

It was a

howling

success.

What does the Were-rabbit do at Christmas? It dresses up as Santa Claws.

How can you tell the Were-rabbit from a normal rabbit?

It's hare-rier.

What should you do if you ever see the Were-rabbit?
Run as fur away as possible.

Why was the Were-rabbit standing on the road?
It was hutch-hiking.

What's the Were-rabbit's favourite day of the week?

Moonday.

What's the Were-rabbit's second favourite day of the week?

Chews-day.

Why does the Were-rabbit have a bath before it goes out?

So it can make a clean getaway.

How does the Were-rabbit go on holiday? By scare-plane.

Why does the Were-rabbit hang out in gardens?
It enjoys ripping things to sheds.

WHAT DID ONE WERE RABBIT SAY TO THE OTHER? 'HOWL YOU DOING?'

What did the Were-rabbit say when it was caught?

'It's a fur cop.'

Why is the Were-rabbit like a footballer? They both dribble a lot.

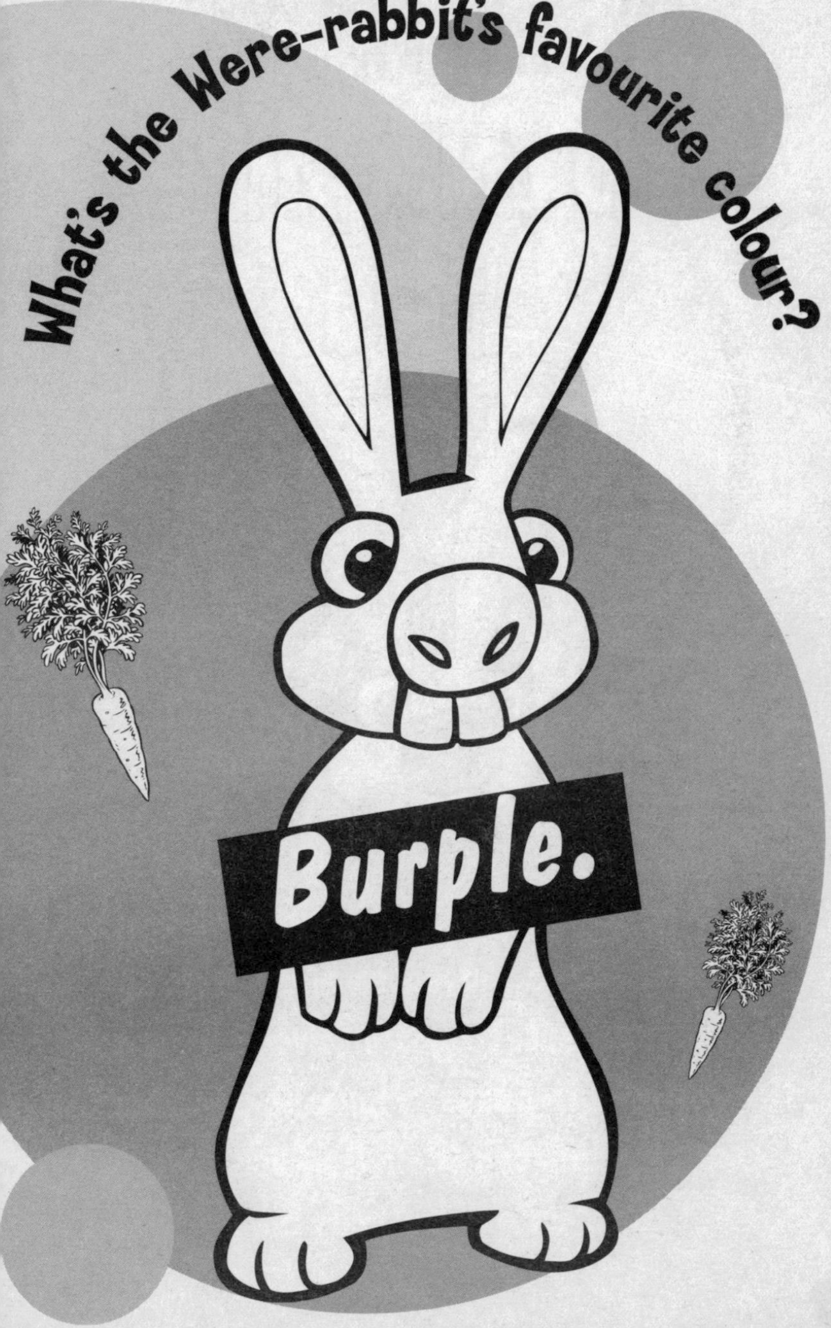
What's the Were-rabbit's favourite colour?
Burple.

THE DYNAMIC DUO

It's time for Wallace, the weight-watching, cheese-loving inventor and his clever canine, Gromit, to get involved! Together they form Anti-pesto, a humane pest-control company, but can their Bun-Vac invention suck up a monstrous bunny?

Why did Wallace and Gromit start a rabbit-catching business?
It seemed like a great hop-portunity.

How do the rabbits feel about being caught?
They were hopping mad.

What do you get if you cross Wallace with a bunny rabbit?
Lots of hare-brained ideas.

Why did Wallace invent the Bun-Vac?
He's a sucker for a new invention.

How does Gromit stop the Bun-Vac? He just presses 'Paws'.

Why is Wallace's van good for transporting rabbits? It's ideal for short hops.

17

Why is Gromit good at solving mysteries?
He always **follows leads.**

Who is Wallace's favourite
relative?
Auntie Pesto.

Why does
Gromit have such
strong opinions?

He's no
door-mutt.

Is Gromit good at telling
stories?

No, he only has one tail.

What does Gromit have in common with Wallace's tummy?
They sometimes growl unexpectedly.

Have you heard about Wallace's new diet? it's flab-ulous.

What's Wallace's idea of paradise? The Garden of Edam.

Do Wallace and Gromit enjoy
the same kinds of cheese?
Well, grate minds
think alike.

Why does Gromit keep staring at Wallace?

He's watching his weight.

What does Wallace put on his toast in the morning? Middle-age spread.

MIDDLE AGE SPREAD

What did Wallace say before he ate the slab of cheese?

'Let's not go to waist.'

PROTECTED BY ANTI-PESTO

What's Wallace up to today? He's on a fat-finding mission.

Why did Wallace go on a diet?
He wanted a new weigh of life.

Why didn't he start sooner?
I don't know, but it was worth the weight.

24

Why did Wallace throw his wallet away?

He wanted to lose a few pounds.

Why does Wallace eat so much cheese at Christmas?

Because there are so many crackers around.

THE FEARFUL FOOD

While West Wallaby's residents rush out to lock up their veggies, Wallace and Gromit have come up with a plan. Can they catch the Were-rabbit before it makes a meal of the town's yummy veg?

What did the beans do when the Were-rabbit came for them?

They did a runner.

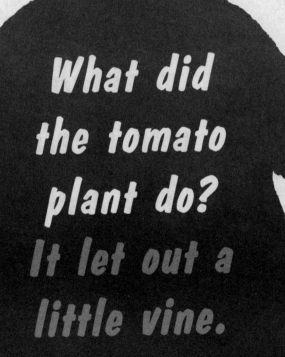

What did the tomato plant do? It let out a little vine.

How did the peas react? They were frozen to the spot.

Which vegetable wet itself? The leek.

Which vegetable can't be bothered to hide from the Were-rabbit? The couch potato.

What did the vegetables say when they saw the Were-rabbit? 'Leaf us alone!'

Why did the Were-rabbit destroy the vegetable patch?
It's a complete howligan.

Why is the Were-rabbit hiding among the beans?
It's stalking them.

Why is the Were-rabbit always hungry?

It's got a big hoppetite.

How does the Were-rabbit like its snacks?

Bite-size.

31

What's the Were-rabbit's favourite country? Gnaw-way.

What does the Were-rabbit say before it runs into a garden?

'Veggie, steady, go!'

How did the Were-rabbit get all the vegetables home?
In a wheel-burrow.

What did the Were-rabbit say to the carrot?
'It's been nice gnawing you.'

Why did the Were-rabbit avoid the playground?
It's a no-grow area.

33

When do Were-rabbits eat the most carrots?

Crunchtime.

Did you hear the one about the Were-rabbit who ate a sofa and an armchair?
It had a suite tooth.

Did you hear the one about the Were-rabbit who ate a cauliflower and a jelly?
It got the collywobbles.

Did you hear the one about the
Were-rabbit who ate the melted ice cream?

It soon licked it into shape.

Did you hear the one about the sick Were-rabbit?
It's howl right now.

When is the Giant Vegetable
Competition being held?

To-marrow.

36

What do you call an oversized vegetable?

A plumpkin.

Why can't Wallace fit pumpkin in his van? It's too much of a squash.

What hides in the garden shed and trembles?

A nervous rake.

What do you get if you cross a garden tool with the Were-rabbit?

A tr-oooooooowwww-el.

THE VILE VICTOR

Just when things couldn't get any worse
for Wallace and Gromit, there's a visit
from Victor Quartermaine. Proud,
pompous and addicted to hunting,
Victor's determined to take a shot at the
Were-rabbit as soon as he can.

Why did Victor draw rabbits on his bald head?

He thought they would look like hares from a distance.

What's the difference between a burglar and Victor Quartermaine?
One has false keys,
the other has false locks.

What's Victor's mission in life?
To baldly go where no man has gone before.

42

What's Victor's favourite story? Baldilocks.

What happened when Victor lost his wig? The police combed the area.

HOW DOES VICTOR KEEP HIS EARS WARM IN WINTER? WITH AN EARWIG.

What does Victor really
want to be?
A hair-istocrat.

When does Victor shoot
naughty rabbits?
On a bad hare day.

Why did
Victor
take up
hunting?
He'll give
anything a shot.

Why was the Were-rabbit pleased to see Victor's trousers fall down?

It likes a full moon.

THE TERRIFIED TOWNSFOLK

The residents of West Wallaby are shaking in their shoes – the Were-rabbit is still on the loose. Lady Tottington wants to give Wallace and Gromit a second chance. Can they save the day?

What kind of sounds do the townsfolk
fear most?
Things that go crunch in the night.

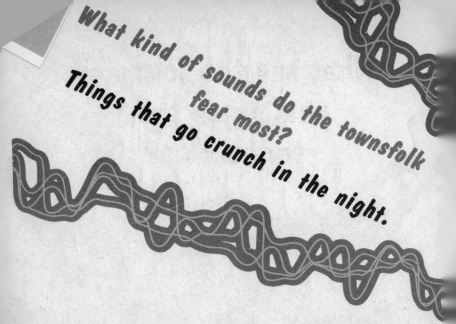

Do they go to the cinema?
Yes: for the big scream.

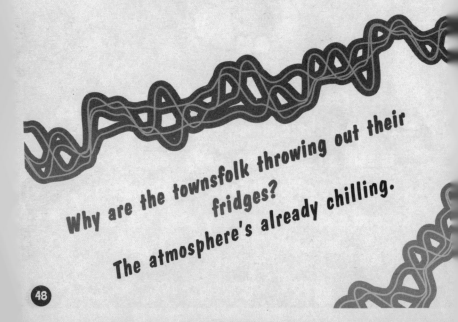

Why are the townsfolk throwing out their
fridges?
The atmosphere's already chilling.

What are the townsfolk putting on their vegetables?

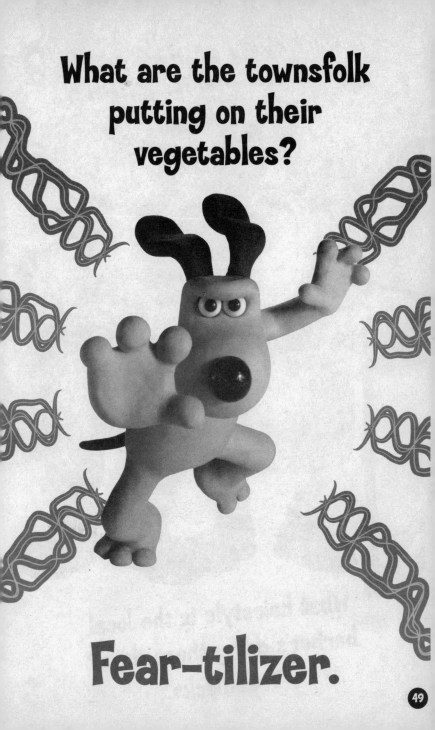

Fear-tilizer.

What do you get if you cross a townsperson with the local puss?
A scaredy-cat.

What hairstyle is the local barber's doing these days?
Dreadlocks.

Why are the townsfolk hiding
in the recycling plant?
They're into eek-ology.

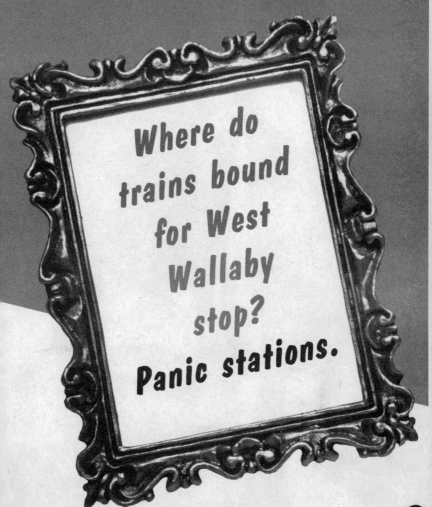

Where do
trains bound
for West
Wallaby
stop?
Panic stations.

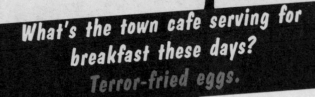

What's the town cafe serving for breakfast these days?
Terror-fried eggs.

What's the cafe serving for lunch? Shake-and-kidney pie.

52

What's for dessert?
Cowardy custard.

Why is the vicar scared of the Were-rabbit?
He thinks the beast might
pray upon him.

Why did the vicar tremble when he saw the Were-rabbit? He couldn't sermon up any courage.

What's the difference between the vicar and the church?

One's a hysterical sight, the other's a historical site.

54

Why will the vicar always be scared of the beast? You can't altar his mind.

What did PC Mackintosh say when he saw the Were-rabbit?

'I want the truth, the howl truth and nothing but the truth.'

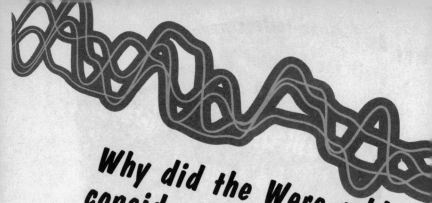

Why did the Were-rabbit consider giving itself up?

A change is as good as arrest.

What do you get if a horde of angry townsfolk storm across a field?

Corn on the mob.

Why do fortune-tellers never visit the town of West Wallaby? They know a terrible fête awaits them.